AUSSIE PUBLISHERS

Beautiful BULLION

The Complete Guide to Bullion Embroidery

By Leisa Pownall

AUSSIE PUBLISHERS

ACKNOWLEDGEMENTS

The source of my greatest inspiration is my wonderful students. Their enthusiasm for learning and unfailing belief that I can do whatever they challenge me with keeps me going.

I would like to thank Aussie Publishers for having the confidence to publish this, my first book. At the same time I would like to personally thank Emma Borghesi for her guidance and patience in editing and producing this book. I would also like to thank my friends at Penguin Threads (Australia) and Madeira (Australia) for supplying me with the wonderful threads and fabrics used throughout my book.

I would also like to thank Julie Ellis for supplying her beautiful Gumnut Yarns and silk; Lesley Mulder, a fantastic student, for sewing up the cushions 'Lover's Garland' and 'Spray of Lavender'; Josie and Paul Nonnis of Bentleigh Framers for framing 'Nicholas's Dreamtime'; and Neil Lorimer for his beautiful photography.

Last but not least, I thank my wonderful and supportive husband Simon and my three beautiful girls Sophie, Phoebe and Hannah. If not for them I would not have picked up a needle and thread.

AUSSIE PUBLISHERS

25-27 Izett Street, Prahran, Victoria 3181 Australia

Website: http://www.penguin-threads.com.au

E-mail: info@penguin-threads.com.au

First published by Aussie Publishers 2000

10 9 8 7 6 5 4 3 2 1

Text, templates and designs copyright ©Leisa Pownall, 2000

Photography copyright ©Aussie Publishers, 2000

This compilation copyright ©Aussie Publishers, 2000

All rights reserved.

Designed and produced by Borghesi & Adam Publishers Pty. Ltd.

Photography by Neil Lorimer

Printed and bound in Singapore

National Library of Australia Cataloguing-in-Publication Data:

Pownall, Leisa.

Beautiful Bullion.

ISBN 1 876364 73 4

1. Bullion work. 2. Embroidery. I. Title.

764.44

Contents

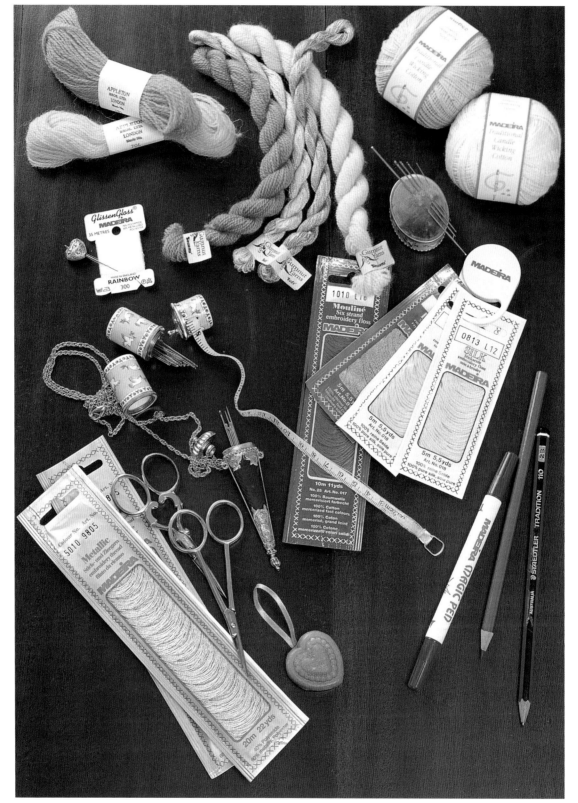

Introduction

This book will help you to create the perfect bullion stitch, and will show you
how to use the stitch in a multitude of designs.
It provides step-by-step instructions on how to do all the stitches used in this kind
of embroidery. I also explain how to choose the right tools, as a lot of people don't realise
that you need different needles for different stitches and threads.

I hope you enjoy this book and become an addicted embroiderer like me!

EQUIPMENT AND TECHNIQUES

Needles

For bullion stitch, french knots and colonial knots, you must use a
straw or milliner's needle, and occasionally a doll needle.

Straw and milliner's needles are the same width from the top to the
bottom. All other needles widen at the eye, which would make it difficult to pull the needle through the 'wraps' on the needle. (In bullion
stitch, the thread is wound around the needle several times to form the
stitch, as shown in the stitch glossary starting on page 81 of this book.
Each time the thread is wound around the needle, it is counted as one
'wrap'.) The width (diameter) of the needle itself will depend on the
width of the thread or yarn you are using. It should be equal to the
width of the thread or yarn.

For example

For 6 strands of cotton, 4 strands of Madeira Silk or 2 strands of crewel
wool you would use a size 1 straw needle.
For 3 strands of cotton or 2 strands of Madeira Silk you would use a
size 7 or 8 straw needle.
For 1 strand of cotton you would use a size 10 straw needle.

Note: If you are a tight embroiderer you may need to go up one size
(the higher the needle number, the finer the needle).

If you are using 6 strands of thread and wrapping more than 24 times you will need to use a doll needle. This is a very long needle and is slightly wider at one end. It should only be used with six strands of thread, or thick wool.

Threads

You can use almost any type of yarn or thread for bullion embroidery. The easiest to use is cotton or silk, while the hardest is metallic or rayon thread.

Finding the Grain

Thread, like fabric, has a grain. If you sew with the thread going against the grain of the fabric, the thread will twist and tangle and wear more quickly. To find the grain, run your fingers down the thread. One direction will feel smoother than the other. Sew with the smooth side running downwards, away from the needle, and with the knot at the bottom.

Tips

- You will only be able to find the grain in this way when the strands of the thread are all together. Once they have separated, you won't be able to feel the difference. Therefore, when you find the grain, knot the bottom straight away, so that when you pick the thread up you will know which is the right way.
- If you need to separate the thread, split it in the direction of the grain and it won't knot or tangle.
- Wool feels furrier the wrong way.
- When using thread that is on a reel, use the end that you pull off the reel to thread through the needle, and place the knot at the end which you cut.
- Never cut thread longer than 40 cm, otherwise it will wear out as you stitch. On a longer piece of thread, the start will be thicker than the end.
- If you are using metallic thread, cut no longer than 30 cm, as this type of thread wears more quickly.

Fabric

The choice of fabric available is limitless. You can use anything, so long as it is suitable for the item you are embroidering.

Tips

· It is a good idea to wash fabric first to allow for any shrinkage.
· Always test marking pens or transfers on a scrap of fabric before using. Many people have been caught when they have been unable to remove the markings from their embroidery.
· Be careful if you are using fabric with a rayon or polyester content, as they do not behave in the same way as natural fabrics.

Scissors

Sharp scissors are the only ones I like to use, so keep them away from handymen and children! Buy a pair that can be unscrewed and properly sharpened when blunt. It is harder to thread a needle with a piece of thread that has been cut with blunt scissors.

Hoops

Working bullion stitch in a hoop is very difficult, so I don't usually recommend it. However, hoops are fantastic for lots of other stitches which you may use in combination with your bullion stitch, particularly the hands-free ones which are now available. If you do use a hoop, always remember not to leave your work in it when you are not working on it.

Transferring Designs

There are several ways you can transfer a design onto a piece of work, and the method you choose will depend on the fabric you are using.

For fabric that is see-through, use transfer pens or pencils, but test them first (see page 8). Tape the design template onto a window, then tape the fabric over the top, with the right side facing up. Now you have a 'light box', and can easily trace the design onto the fabric.

If you can't trace the design onto fabric in this way, try using dressmaker's carbon. Place the fabric onto a firm surface (right side up), and place

the carbon, face down, on top. Next place the design on top of the carbon, and secure it in place with pins so the fabric and design don't move while you are tracing. Use a lead pencil to trace firmly around the design.

Soluble fabric is also a good way to transfer designs. Trace the design onto the soluble fabric then tack the soluble fabric to your work. When you have finished your embroidery, wet the soluble fabric and it will disappear. Fine tissue paper can be used in the same way, and can be torn away (instead of dissolved) when the work is complete.

If none of the above will work, I suggest working out where the larger parts of the design go and marking them in, and then using these as a guide to work your smaller areas. This is a less precise method, but also allows the embroiderer more freedom with the design.

Transfer Pens or Pencils

There is some controversy over fabric pens: to use or not to use! I have used them with both success and failure. The following tips might help you to use them successfully:

Tips

- Always test them on the fabric first and make sure the markings will come out easily.
- Don't iron markings unless the transfer pen instructions tell you to do so, as heat can make the marking permanent (as I discovered).
- A soft lead pencil is often suitable for transferring designs, but again test it first on a scrap.
- The best way to remove markings is to handwash your work in warm, soapy water. Be sure to rinse thoroughly.

· The special transfer pens that produce markings which gradually fade can be great. However, be aware that different things will affect how quickly the markings will fade, so be careful. A marking which fades before you have completed your embroidery can be as much of a problem as a marking which cannot be removed.

Preparing Fabric or a Garment for Embroidery

If you are going to embroider something you are making yourself, don't cut out the fabric until the embroidery is finished. Instead, trace the pattern piece onto the fabric, and leave excess fabric around it. This allows for any fraying and will prevent you from losing part of your pattern. Once the embroidery is finished, you can cut out the pattern accurately.

When embroidering a piece to frame, again leave plenty of excess fabric around the edges, as you will need it for blocking and mounting the work.

If you are embroidering a garment or piece of fabric made from knitted or stretch fabric, or with an open weave, tack a piece of medium weight interfacing to the back of the area to be embroidered. This stops the fabric from stretching while you are working on it. Cut away the excess interfacing as close to the embroidery as possible when it is finished. Where possible hide the back of your work by lining with fabric or ribbon.

Afterwards

Most embroidery is washable, so I suggest washing your piece when you have finished. Even when you think your hands are clean, there will be some traces of dirt left behind when you have finished. I prefer to wash in warm water and with a mild detergent. Rinse until the water is clear, and roll the embroidery in a towel to remove excess water. Press your work while it is still damp. When pressing, place the embroidery face down on a thick towel. This will stop the work from being pressed flat.

Bullion Rules

Before you start embroidering, you need to understand that just as no two people are identical, nor is their embroidery. While the instructions provided in this book are as detailed as they can be, you may need to modify them slightly to suit your personal style. If you are a tight embroiderer, you will probably need more wraps than a pattern dictates and perhaps thicker thread. You may also need a larger needle. If you have trouble pulling the needle through the wraps, you may need to use a bigger needle. The reverse applies if you are a particularly loose embroiderer.

The size of the needle and the thickness of the thread will determine how big or small your bullion stitch will be. The finer the thread and needle the finer the stitch, and conversely the thicker the thread and needle, the bigger the stitch.

I suggest you use the number of bullion wraps specified as a guide only, and learn to determine the number of wraps yourself. For a pattern to be absolutely precise about the number of wraps for a bullion stitch, it would also have to tell you the length of the stitch taken, and this would become too difficult. Instead, you should work in the following way: If you want your bullion to sit straight, with no curve, the wraps on the needle should be the same length as the stitch you have taken. The more you want your bullion to curve, the longer the wraps on the needle in comparison to the length of the stitch you have taken. For example, a small stitch combined with a high number of wraps will create a very curved bullion stitch, as in the bullion loop stitch (see the Stitch Glossary on page 81).

When working bullion stitch, you always wrap the thread around the needle in a clockwise direction, regardless of whether you are left- or right-handed. This helps to stop the thread from twisting. Always keep hold of the wraps when you pull the needle and thread through.

If you find you have wrapped the thread too tightly around the needle, you may not be able to pull the needle through the wraps. If this happens, keep the wraps on the needle but use your thumb to gently roll them backwards (anti-clockwise) on the needle. This will loosen the wraps and enable you to pull the needle through. Once you have pulled the needle through, roll the wraps back the other way to tighten them again. This is also handy if your bullion is too loose; before ending off, tighten the loops by rolling them between your fingers.

Couching

If your bullions are long and curved, you will need to couch them down to both hold them in position, and to help to shape them. Do this by using a single strand of thread the same colour as your bullion. Come up on one side of the bullion and take a stitch over the bullion to the other side (also refer to Couching instructions in the Stitch Glossary on page 81).

figure 1

Side view of a long bullion: Here the bullion is longer than the length of fabric it covers, so it forms a gentle loop.

figure 2

couching

Side view of a long bullion after couching, which holds the bullion down. Couching also helps to shape the bullion (see below).

figure 3

Top view of a long bullion. It will appear slightly curved because the bullion is longer than the length of fabric it covers.

figure 4

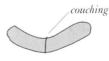
couching

Top view of a long bullion, after couching. This holds the bullion down, and has also been used to shape the bullion .

Spray of Lavender Cushion

This is one of a pair of cushions and would make a gorgeous gift for a special someone.
The second cushion, Lover's Garland, is featured on page 17.

MATERIALS

- 1 m of cream wool challis
- 32 cm cream zip
- Madeira Stranded embroidery cotton
  light green (1701)
  medium green (1702)
  dark green (1705)
  light purple (0801)
  medium purple (0803)
- Cream sewing threads

EQUIPMENT

- Size 7 or 8 straw needle
- Sewing machine

STITCHES USED

- Bullion stitch, stem stitch, straight stitch, herringbone stitch

PREPARATION

Cut one square of fabric 40 cm by 40 cm, then overlock the edges to prevent fraying. Trace the design onto the centre of the fabric, using the middle of the bow as a guide (see template on page 15).

EMBROIDERY

Stems Using three strands of medium green, stem-stitch the stems.

Leaves Using one strand of medium green, work straight-stitch leaves on both sides of the stem.

Lavender Use one strand each of light purple, medium purple and light green threaded into the one needle, and work nine 8-wrap bullion stitches to form the lavender petals as shown in the diagram (figure 1). Work the bullions in the sequence shown in figure 2, starting with *a*.

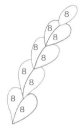

figure 1

Bow Using three strands of dark green, work the bow in herringbone stitch. Work on the left tail first, then the right loop, then the left loop and finally on the right tail.

figure 2

FINISHING

When you have completed the embroidery, cut out the frills for the cushion. You will need to cut three strips each measuring 20 cm by 115 cm. Join the strips right sides together along the 20 cm edges, to form one long strip of about 20 cm by 3.45 m long.

Join the ends to make one continuous piece. Fold in half lengthways, then press. Gather the raw edges together and pull up to measure 148 cm around. This is the frill.

To form the back of the cushion, cut out one new piece of fabric 30 cm by 40 cm and another piece 14.5 cm by 40 cm. Along one long side of the 14.5 cm strip, turn under 3 cm and press. Along one long side of the 30 cm strip, turn under 1.5 cm and press. Insert the zip in between these two pieces of fabric, with the right side of the zip under the fold of the 28 cm by 40 cm piece and the left side of the zip under the 13 cm by 40 cm piece. This piece overlaps the bigger piece by 1 cm. You will now have a piece 40 cm by 40 cm. Sew the frill to the embroidered piece, raw edges together. Then join to the back piece, right sides together. Machine stitch 1.5cm in from the edge all the way around. Leave zipper open for turning the pillow out.

SPRAY OF LAVENDER CUSHION TEMPLATE—100%

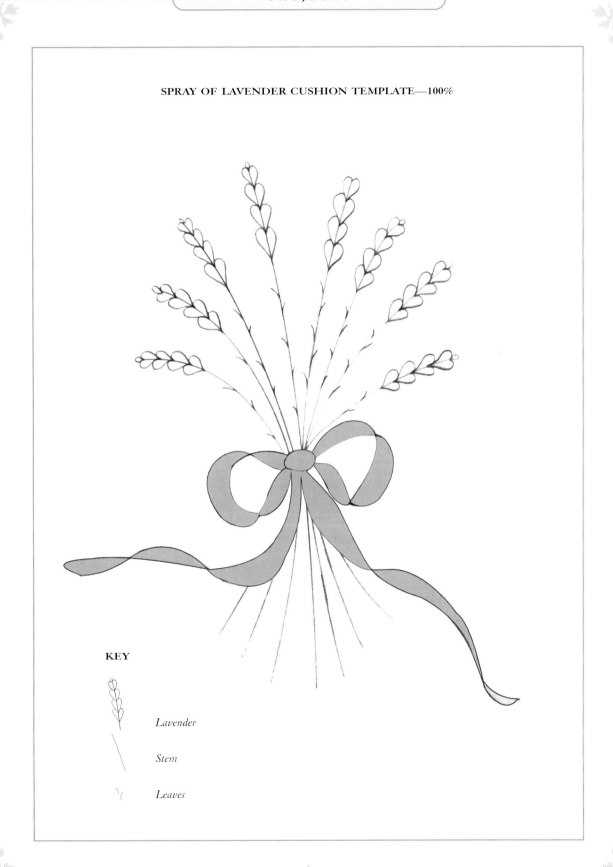

KEY

Lavender

Stem

Leaves

Lovers' Garland Cushion

This delicate cushion, featured on page 16, is the pair to the Spray of Lavender cushion on page 12. They look lovely together, and also on their own.

MATERIALS

- · 1 m cream wool challis
- · 32 cm cream zip
- · Gumnut Daisies wool
  blue (344)
  light yellow (743)
  dark yellow (745)
  light pink (050)
  dark pink (176)
  cream (991)
  green (643)
- · Cream sewing thread

EQUIPMENT

- · Size 7 straw needle
- · Sewing machine

STITCHES USED

- · Bullion stitch, bullion loop stitch, french knot, fly stitch, lazy daisy stitch, satin stitch, stem stitch.

PREPARATION

Cut a square of fabric 40 cm by 40 cm and overlock the edges. Using the template on page 20, trace the design onto the centre and place the centre of the bow 16 cm up from the bottom edge of the fabric.

Shaping forget-me-nots:

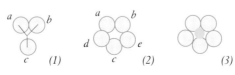

Using french knots, work in the form of a letter Y with a and b touching (1). Add knots between a and c then b and c (2) then add one knot to the centre (3).

EMBROIDERY

Bow   Using two strands of blue, satin-stitch the bow.

Garland   Using one strand of green, stem-stitch the garland circle. Work lazy daisy leaves on the ends where the circle nearly meets.

figure 1

Large daisies   Using one strand of light pink, work each petal with two 5-wrap bullions side by side (see figure 1). Work five petals. Using one strand of dark pink, do three 1-wrap french knots for the centre. Also refer to 'Shaping daisies' instructions below.

figure 2

Small Daisies   Using one strand of light yellow, work five petal daisies in lazy daisy stitch. There will be some with just two or three petals and a centre. Using one strand of dark yellow, work a 1-wrap french knot in the centre. Also refer to 'Shaping daisies' instructions below.

figure 3

Forget-me-nots   Using one strand of blue, work five petal forget-me-nots with 1-wrap french knots. Using one strand of light yellow, work 1-wrap french knots in the centres. Also refer to 'Shaping forget-me-nots' instructions on page 17.

Rose buds   Using one strand of cream, work each bud with two 5-wrap bullions side by side (figure 2). Using one strand of green, work a fly stitch around each bullion.

Bullion loop daisies   Using one strand of dark pink, work three 10-wrap bullion loops for each flower (figure 3). Also refer to 'Shaping daisies' instructions below.

Leaves   Using one strand of green, work lazy daisy leaves in amongst the flowers.

Shaping daisies:

To shape 5-petal daisies worked in bullion or lazy daisy stitch, work in the form of a letter Y (1), then put petals in between a and c then b and c (2). Add a centre if required (3).

Detail: Lovers' Garland cushion

FINISHING

When you have completed the embroidery, cut out frills for the cushion. You will need to cut three strips 20 cm by the width of the fabric (approximately 115 cm). Join the strips right sides together to form one long strip of about 3.45 m long. Join the ends to make it one piece. Fold in half lengthways and press. Gather raw edges together and pull up to measure 148 cm around.

Cut out one piece of fabric 30 cm by 40 cm and one piece 14.5 cm by 40 cm. These will form the back of the cushion. Along one long side of the 14.5 cm strip, turn under 3 cm and press. Along one long side of the 30 cm strip, turn under 1.5 cm and press. Insert the zip in between these two pieces of fabric, with the right side of the zip under the fold of the 28 cm by 40 cm piece and the left side of the zip under the 13 cm by 40 cm. This piece overlaps the bigger piece by 1cm. You will now have a piece 40 cm by 40 cm. Sew the frill to the embroidered piece, raw edges together. Then join to the back piece, right sides together. Machine-stitch 1.5 cm in from the edge all the way around. Leave zipper open for turning the pillow out.

LOVERS' GARLAND TEMPLATE—100%

KEY

Large daisies

Small daisies
(note: some will need only 2 or 3 petals

Bullion loop daisies

Forget-me-nots

Rose buds

Leaves

Heavenly Lavender Heart

*This cushion looks great amongst a pile of cushions and the delicate scent of lavender
will fill your bedroom.*

MATERIALS

- 35 cm x 40 cm cream wool blanket
- 40 cm x 50 cm cream batiste
- Fibre filling
- 1 m lavender cord
- 100 g dried lavender
- Madeira candlewicking thread in green, cream and lavender
- Madeira Decora Floss
  cream (1482)
  lavender(1511)
- Cream and lavender sewing thread

Detail: Heavenly Lavender Heart

EQUIPMENT

· Size 1 straw needle
· Sewing machine

STITCHES USED

· Bullion stitch, french knot, stem stitch, straight stitch

PREPARATION

Using the template on page 24, trace the heart shape onto some thick paper and cut it out. Then trace around this to transfer the design onto the wool blanket. Mark in stems and lavender.

EMBROIDERY

Stems   Using one strand of green candlewicking thread, stem-stitch the heart, then the stems, to form the lavender.

Lavender   Using one strand each of lavender Decora Floss and lavender candlewicking floss threaded into the straw needle, work nine 8-wrap bullions for each lavender head.

Leaves   Using one strand of green, work straight-stitch leaves either side of the stems.

Cream Flowers   Using one strand each of cream Decora Floss and cream candlewicking floss threaded into a size 1 straw needle, work three 1-wrap french knots in a cluster for each flower.

FINISHING

Cut out the wool heart. Cut out the backing piece. Put right sides together and machine-stitch around the heart outline with the cream sewing thread. Leave a small opening to turn right sides out and to stuff. Stuff cushion with lavender and fibre-fill. Slip-stitch the opening closed. Using slip-stitch, attach the cord around the edge of heart with lavender sewing thread.

HEAVENLY LAVENDER HEART TEMPLATE—90%

(Enlarge to 111% to restore to full size)

KEY

Cream flowers

Lavender

Stem and leaves

Beautiful Bows

This beautiful cardigan would be equally suited for a child or an adult. You can use any type of jumper or cardigan. Go wild and add as many or few bows as you want!

MATERIALS

- Cream cardigan
- Madeira Silk floss
  pink (0502)
  blue (1001)
  green (1701)
  yellow (0112)
  white (2401)

EQUIPMENT

- Size 1 straw needle

STITCHES USED

- Bullion stitch, bullion loop stitch, french knot, couching

PREPARATION

Using a fabric pen, mark the placement of the bows by putting a dot on the cardigan where the centre of each bow will go. Create a random but elegant pattern with the bows, using as many or as few as you like.

BEAUTIFUL BOWS TEMPLATE—100%

(Repeat the bows in a random pattern over the garment, as seen in the photograph on page 27)

EMBROIDERY

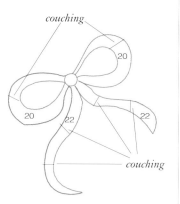

figure 1

Each bow is worked in four strands of silk with a size 1 straw needle. Use different colours (pink, blue, green, yellow and white) to suit your design, as shown in the photograph.

Work a 20-wrap bullion loop to the left of the centre. Work a 20-wrap bullion loop to the right of the centre. There should be a 2mm gap in between the two loops. Work a 1-wrap french knot in the centre. Work a 22-wrap bullion stitch for each tail. Start the bullion tails at the centre of the bow. This is so you can pull the bullions tighter at the end, so the ends of the bow tails are thinner than the start (figure 1).

To shape the tails, couch with one strand of silk (the same colour as the bow you have just worked). Catch each bullion tail in two places. You can make the tails curve any way you like. Couch the bullion loops, with one strand of silk, so they sit flat on the fabric.

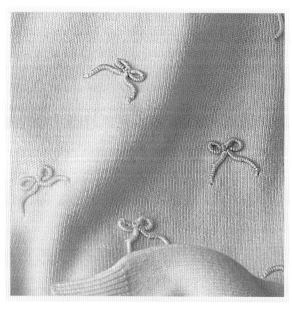

Detail: Beautiful Bows

Simply Sweet

A plain cardigan is transformed with the addition of hand-embroidered flowers around the neck and down the front.

MATERIALS

- Cream cardigan
- Madeira Stranded embroidery cotton in
  pink (0501)
  white (2401)
  blue (1001)
  yellow (0112)

EQUIPMENT

- Size 7 or 8 straw needle

STITCHES USED

- Bullion stitch, french knot

PREPARATION

Mark the centre of each daisy and forget-me-not onto the cardigan, using the template on page 31 as a guide. I have placed the daisies around the neck approximately 6 cm apart with the forget-me-nots placed half-way between each one. The daisies going down the front are placed between the buttons and are about 5 cm apart. I have placed each forget-me-knot half-way between a button and a daisy. If, however, you are using a different style or size cardigan, you may need to vary the placement of the flowers accordingly.

EMBROIDERY

figure 1

All the embroidery is worked in three strands of thread.

Daisies Using white thread and a size 7 straw needle, work the centres of the daisies first. The outside bullions are 9 wraps each and the centre bullion is 7 wraps (figure 1). Using pink thread, work eight bullion bud petals around the centre bullions. There are two bullions for each petal and these are 7 wraps each. To shape the daisy, work four petals in a cross shape (see below), then fit the remaining four between the first four.

Forget-me-nots Using blue thread, work five 1-wrap french knots in a cluster. Using yellow thread, work a 1-wrap french knot in the centre of the blue knots. Also refer to 'Shaping forget-me-nots' instructions on page 17.

Remember to end each flower off individually; do not carry the thread across the back of work.

Shaping 7-petal daisies:

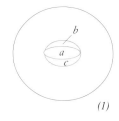

(1)

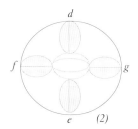

(2)

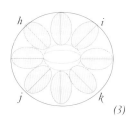

(3)

Mark a circle on the fabric as a guide, then work the centre of the daisy in the middle of the circle, as shown. Work a first, then b then c (1). Next, work four petals in a cross around the centre (2). Finally, add the remaining four petals in between the first four petals, as shown (3).

SIMPLY SWEET TEMPLATE—65%

(Enlarge to 154% to restore to full size)

KEY

Daisies

Forget-me-nots

Blue by You

This delicate towel will have your friends green with envy.

MATERIALS

- Emma Taylor blue hand towel
- Madeira Stranded embroidery cotton
  dark pink (0809)
  medium pink (2610)
  light pink (0808)
  green (1512)
- Blue ribbon 4 cm x 48 cm
- Blue sewing thread to match ribbon

EQUIPMENT

- Size 7 straw needle

STITCHES USED

- Bullion stitch, fly stitch, lazy daisy stitch, stem stitch, straight stitch

PREPARATION

Using the template (page 34), transfer the design using dress-maker's carbon. Alternatively, mark the centre on the towel, then work the rest of the design.

EMBROIDERY

Stems Work stem stitch in two strands of green.

Roses Using three strands of dark pink, work three bullions for each centre. The outside two have 9 wraps and the centre 7. Use three strands of medium pink to work five bullions around the centre three. The first will have 9 wraps, the second 11, the third 13, and the fourth and fifth will have 15 each. Using three strands of light pink, work seven 15-wrap bullions around the medium bullions. The first diagram shows the number of wraps; the second the sequence (figure 1).

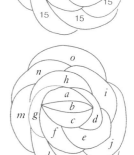

figure 1

Detail: Blue by You

Rose Buds   Using three strands of light pink, work the outside of the buds first. These two bullions have 7 wraps each. Using three strands of dark pink, work the centres with a 5-wrap bullion (figure 2). Using two strands of green, work a fly stitch around the entire bud. Then work a second fly stitch, half way down the bud around the first. Work a straight stitch from the base of the bud into the centre of the dark pink bullion.

figure 2

Leaves   Using two strands of green, work lazy daisy leaves either side of the stem, amongst the buds.

FINISHING

Slip stitch or machine stitch a piece of ribbon across the back of towel. This will cover the back of the work and also looks quite pretty.

BLUE BY YOU TEMPLATE—100%

KEY   *Roses*

Stem

Rose buds

Leaves

Colourful Camellias

This bright but simple towel will brighten your bathroom.
See photograph on page 35.

See photograph on page 35.

MATERIALS

- · Emma Taylor white hand towel
- · Madeira Stranded embroidery cotton
  dark pink (0703)
  medium pink (0701)
  light pink (0613)
  green (1408)
- · 4 cm x 48 cm white or pink ribbon
- · Sewing thread to match ribbon

EQUIPMENT

- · Size 1 straw needle

STITCHES USED

- · Bullion loop stitch, french knot

Shaping large camellias:

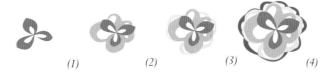

(1)   *(2)*   *(3)*   *(4)*

Work the three bullion stitches in the centre first, using the deepest pink (1).
Next, work five bullion loops in the medium pink (2).
Then work seven bullion loops in the lightest pink (3). Finally, add nine bullion loops in green (4).

PREPARATION

Mark the centre of the towel band with a dot (a). Next mark two dots (b and c) 4 cm either side of a. Now mark two more dots (d and e) 3 cm either side of b and c.

e •   c •   a •   b •   d •

3 cm   4 cm   4 cm   3 cm

EMBROIDERY

All the embroidery is worked in six strands of cotton and a size 1 straw needle.

Large Flowers   Using dark pink cotton, work the centre of the flower with three 18-wrap bullion loops. Using medium pink cotton, work five 20-wrap bullion loops around the first three. Using light pink, work seven 22-wrap bullion loops around the medium pink loops. Using green thread, work nine 24-wrap bullion loops around the light pink loops (figure 1). Also refer to 'Shaping large camellias' on page 36.

Small Flowers   Using dark pink, work three 18-wrap bullion loops. Work a 1-wrap dark pink french knot in the centre of the loops. Using green, work five 20-wrap bullion loops around the centre three (figure 2).

FINISHING

Slip-stitch or machine stitch the ribbon across the back of the towel band.

figure 1:

Work three 18-wrap bullion loops in dark pink; work five 20-wrap bullion loops in medium pink; work seven 22-wrap bullion loops in light pink; work nine 24-wrap bullion loops in green.

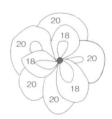

figure 2:

The 18-wrap bullion loops in dark pink with a 1-wrap french knot added to the centre. The five 20-wrap bullion loops are worked in green.

COLOURFUL CAMELLIAS TEMPLATE—50%

(Enlarge to 200% to restore to full size)

KEY   *Small camellia*

Large camellia

Ray of Sunshine

*Waffle is big and these sunflowers worked on black ribbon on a hand towel and face washer
will have your stylish friends clamoring for more.*

MATERIALS

- White waffle hand towel
- White waffle face washer
- Black ribbon to fit across the bottom of the towel and face washer. (I bought mine with the ribbon already stitched on. However it would be easier to work on the ribbon first before stitching onto the towel.)
- Size 7 straw needle
- Madeira Stranded embroidery cotton
  yellow (0113)
  green (1314)
  orange (0204)
- Madeira Metallic thread 9805
  black-gold (5014)
  gold (5012)

EQUIPMENT

- Size 7 straw needle

STITCHES USED

- Bullion lazy daisy, french knot, stem stitch, lazy daisy stitch

PREPARATION

Using dressmaker's carbon and the template on page 40 as a guide, transfer the design onto the ribbon. You can simply use a large circle to mark the position of each sunflower, then place a smaller circle in the middle of each to mark the centre of the flower.

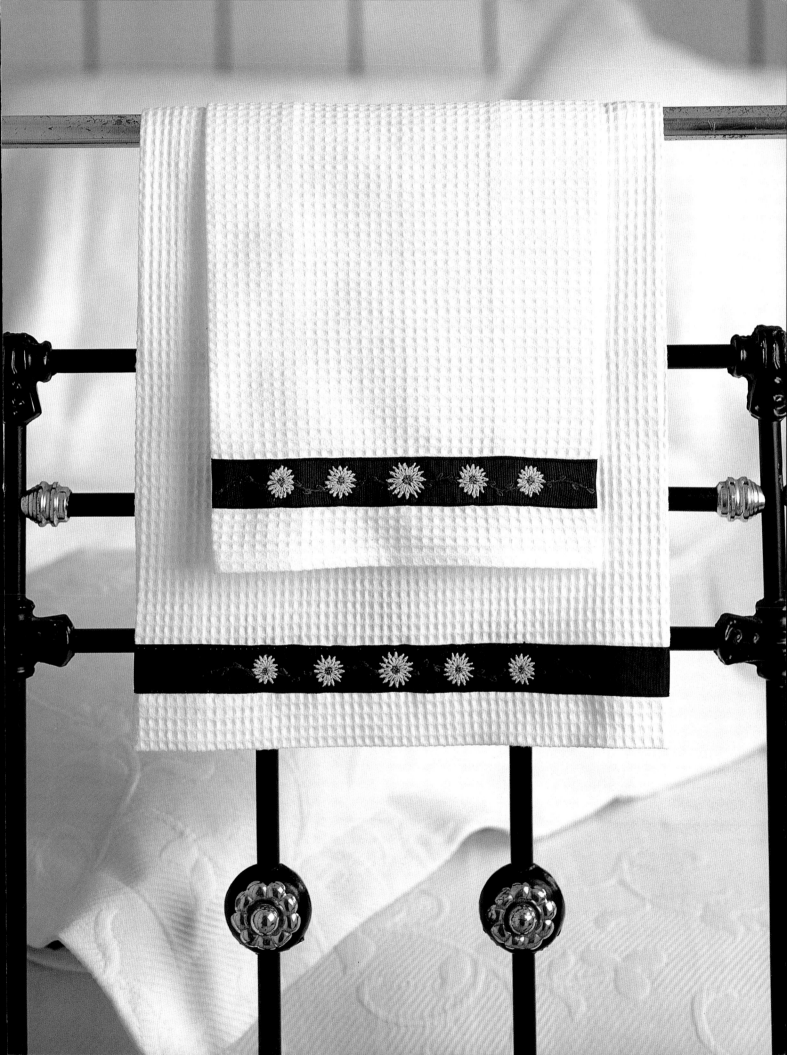

EMBROIDERY

Sunflowers Using three strands of yellow mixed with one strand of gold, work the 16 petals in lazy daisy bullion stitch. Work the first four petals in a cross. Start from the outside edge of the inner circle and take a stitch to the edge of the large circle. Work another four petals half - way between the first four. Work the remaining eight petals, with one each side of the first eight (see 'Shaping the sunflowers' below). Using one strand of orange mixed with two strands of black-gold, fill the centre of the sunflower with 1-wrap french knots.

Stems Using three strands of green, stem-stitch in between the sunflowers.

Leaves Using three strands of green, work the leaves in lazy daisy stitch.

Shaping the sunflowers:

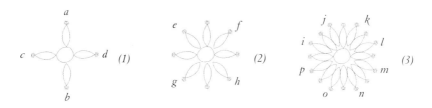

Work the first four petals in the shape of a cross, as shown. Work a first, then b then c then d (1). Now work the next four petals, e, f, g and h, half-way between the first four petals (2). Finally, add the remaining eight petals in between, as shown (3).

FINISHING

Slip-stitch or machine-stitch the ribbon to the fabric 2.5 cm from the bottom edge of towel or face washer. If machine-stitching, thread the top of the machine in black thread and the bobbin in white thread.

RAY OF SUNSHINE TEMPLATE—65%

(Enlarge to 154% to restore to full size)

KEY *Sunflower*

Stem and leaves

Romantic Rug

This blanket would make a gorgeous knee rug or a cot blanket. A timeless design.

MATERIALS

- 75 cm x 105 cm cream doctor's flannel
- 80 cm x 110 cm cotton floral
- 4 m x 7 cm cream cotton lace
- 3.8 m cream cotton entredeux
- 6.5 m of 3 mm double-sided pink ribbon to match thread
- Madeira Stranded embroidery cotton
  light green (1511)
  medium green (1512)
  light pink (0815)
  medium pink (0813)
  dark pink (0812)
- Cream sewing cotton

EQUIPMENT

- Size 1 and size 7 straw needles
- Sewing machine

STITCHES USED

- Bullion stitch, fly stitch, lazy daisy stitch, stem stitch, straight stitch

PREPARATION

The template for this project can be found on the pull-out sheet at the back of this book. Trace the design onto the fabric using a light box or sunny window, placing the oval in the centre of the blanket. The ends of the oval are 35 cm from the short edge of the blanket. The large roses are 3.5 cm in from each corner.

EMBROIDERY

All the bullion stitches are worked in six strands of cotton with a size 1 straw needle.

Roses Using dark pink thread, work the centre of the roses. Work two 7-wrap bullions side by side. Using the medium pink thread, work one 9-wrap bullion, one 11-wrap bullion, one 13-wrap bullion and two 15-wrap bullions. Using the light pink thread, work seven 15-wrap bullions around the medium pink bullion stitches (figure 1). Figure 2 shows the sequence. Start at *a*.

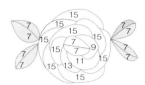

figure 1

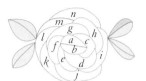

figure 2

Leaves Work two leaves either side of the roses around the edge of blanket. Each leaf has two bullions. Using light green thread, work two bullion stitches side by side, 7 wraps each (figure 1).

Light rose buds Using three strands of light pink, work the outside petals with two 11-wrap bullions. Add the centre, using one 9-wrap bullion stitch, worked in medium pink. Using three strands of light green, work a fly stitch around each bud, then a second fly stitch around the first, but slightly smaller. Work a straight stitch from the base of the bud into the centre (figure 3).

figure 3

Stems, light rose buds Using three strands of light green thread and a size 7 straw needle, stem-stitch the oval and the stems of the longer (lighter) bullion buds around the edge of the blanket (figure 4). Also use the template on the pull-out sheet at the back of this book as a guide.

figure 4:
The lighter bud with leaves.

figure 1

Leaves, light rose buds Using three strands of thread and a size 7 straw needle, work lazy daisy stitch leaves either side of the stems.

Dark Rose Buds Using dark pink thread, work the outside petals with two 9-wrap bullion stitches and one 7-wrap bullion for the centre. Using two strands of dark green and a size 7 straw needle, work two fly stitches around the buds. Take a straight stitch from the base of the bud into the centre (figure 1).

Stems, dark rose buds Using two strands of dark green, stem-stitch the stems (figure 2).

Leaves, dark rose buds Using two strands of dark green, work lazy daisy leaves either side of the stems.

FINISHING

Turn under a 2.5 cm hem around the cotton floral, then press.

Join the lace with a french seam end to end. Gather just the corners slightly, to fit around the blanket. Start with the join in a corner, place lace and flannel, right sides together, with the lace 2 mm in from the edge of the blanket and pin together. Adjust gathers to fit. Tack and then remove pins. I used a rolled hem stitch to join the two together. This is a wide but close-together zig zag. You zig into the heading of the lace and zag over the edge of the blanket and this creates a roll.

Machine stitch the entredeux to the right side of blanket, close to the lace. Mitre the corners (fold at a 45 degree angle and tuck under). Insert ribbon, using a large tapestry needle. Make four bows with the excess ribbon and hand-stitch to the corners.

Place floral print and blanket wrong sides together, pin then tack. Remove pins and machine stitch together, working with the top of the blanket facing up. I stitched around the edge of the entredeux.

figure 2:

The darker bud with leaves.

To Lee-ann with Love

*Make this bright and fresh dressing gown as a gift for a dear friend,
and you will make a friend for life!*

MATERIALS

- White cotton waffle dressing gown
  (You could make your own if you're handy)
- Madeira Silk
  light pink (0502)
  medium pink (0503)
  dark pink (0504)
  green (1510)
  cream (2404)
- Gumnut Silk Stars
  lavender (297)
  *This is a variegated thread; if unavailable, substitute
  a similar colour from the Madeira Silk range.
  This will not be variegated.*
- Gumnut Silk Buds
  blue (365)
  green (584)
  light yellow (744)
  dark yellow (745)

EQUIPMENT

- Size 1 and size 7 straw needles

STITCHES USED

- Bullion stitch, bullion loop stitch, feather stitch, fly stitch, straight
  stitch, stem stitch, lazy daisy stitch, french knot, colonial knot

PREPARATION

If making the gown yourself, trace the design onto the fabric and work
the embroidery before making-up the gown. I would use dressmaker's
carbon or soluble fabric if using a purchased gown.

EMBROIDERY

Large roses Use four strands of the Madeira Silk and a size 1 straw needle. Using dark pink Silk, work the centre of the roses with two 7-wrap bullion stitches side by side. Work one 5-wrap bullion stitch in the centre. Using medium pink Silk, work one 9-wrap bullion stitch, one 11-wrap bullion stitch, one 13-wrap bullion stitch and two 15-wrap bullion stitches. The seven outside petals are all worked in the light pink and 15-wrap bullion stitches (figure 1).

figure 1

Large rose leaves Using one strand of light green Silk and a size 7 straw needle, work pairs of 9-wrap bullions to form the leaves.

figure 2

Rose buds Use four strands of the Madeira Silk and a size 1 straw needle. The smaller buds are two 9-wrap bullion stitches worked side by side in the medium pink. In the dark pink, work a 7-wrap bullion stitch in the centre (figure 2). The larger buds are also worked in four strands of Silk and the size 1 straw needle. In dark pink, work a 7-wrap bullion stitch. Using the medium pink, work a 9-wrap bullion stitch either side of the centre. Using the light pink, work two 7-wrap bullion stitches, either side of the last two, starting half way on the sides.

figure 3

Lavender Using three strands of Gumnut Silk Stars lavender and a size 7 straw needle, work seven 7-wrap bullion stitches to form lavender petals, as shown in the diagram (figure 4).

figure 4

Stems Using two strands of Madeira green Silk and a size 7 straw needle, stem-stitch the stems of the buds. Work two fly stitches around the buds, the second slightly smaller than the first. Take a straight stitch into the centre of the bud from the base. Work lazy daisy leaves either side of the stems.

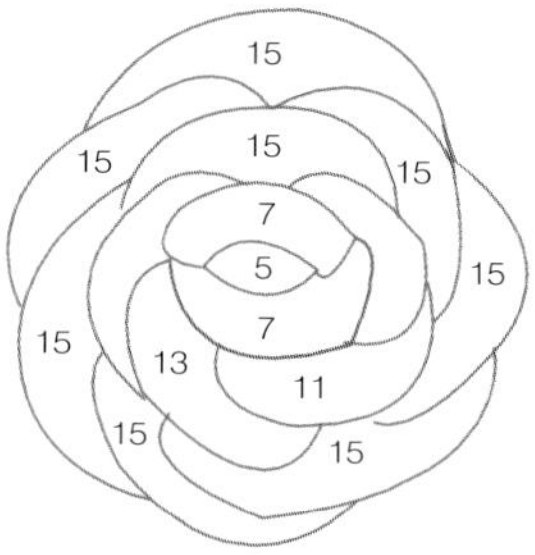

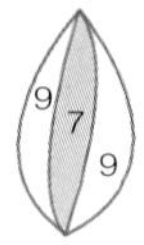

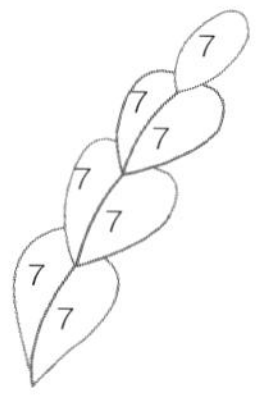

Daisies   Using one strand of blue Silk and a size 7 straw needle, work four 10-wrap bullion loop stitches (figure 1). Using one strand of light yellow Silk, work a 1-wrap french knot in the centre.

figure 1

Small Roses   Using one strand of dark yellow Silk and a size 7 straw needle, work three 6-wrap bullion stitches side by side. Using light yellow Silk, work two 8-wrap bullion stitches just underneath, starting halfway up the sides of the darker bullions and finishing at the centre of the base. Just under these work another two 8-wrap bullions in light yellow (figure 2).

figure 2

Baby's Breath   Using one strand of light green Silk, work feather stitch. Using two strands of cream Silk, work colonial knots in amongst the feather stitches.

Greenery   Using one strand of light green Silk, work fly stitches on the yellow roses and the bases of the lavender.

FINISHING

If you are making your own gown, make up according to the pattern.

TEMPLATE KEY

 Large rose

 Small rose

 Small rose buds

 Lavender

 Daisies

 Baby's breath

 Stem and leaves

 Large rose buds

TO LEE-ANN WITH LOVE TEMPLATE—65%

(Enlarge to 154% to restore to full size)

Sheepish Wheat Bag

*What a wonderful invention. Just pop in the microwave for a few moments and you have an
instant heat pack. I put whole cloves in with the wheat, giving it a lovely aroma.*
Note: *Be careful not to overheat the bag.*

MATERIALS

- 50 cm x 20 cm doctor's flannel
- Madeira Stranded Silk in
  light pink (0502)
  medium pink (0503)
  dark pink (0504)
  white (2401)
  yellow (0112)
  light green (1510)
  dark green (1508)
  gold (2208)
- Madeira Stranded embroidered cotton in
  light purple (0802)
  dark purple (0803)
  green (1702)
- Appletons crewel wool in
  cream
  black (993)
  light green (541)
  dark green (542) blue (876)
- 1kilo of wheat
- 50 gms whole cloves
- 1.6 m of 5 mm pale pink braid
- 1.6 m of 5 mm bright pink braid

EQUIPMENT

- Size 1 and 9 straw needles
- Size 7 or 8 crewel needle
- Cream sewing cotton
- Sewing machine

STITCHES USED

- Bullion stitch, pinwheel blanket stitch, couching, fly stitch, french knot, lazy daisy stitch, pistil stitch, satin stitch, straight stitch,

PREPARATION

Trace the design onto the fabric using a lightbox or sunny window.

TEMPLATE KEY

- Small daisies
- Large daisies
- Grass
- Yellow flowers
- Hollyhocks
- Leaves
- Lavender

SHEEPISH WHEAT BAG—90%

(Enlarge to 111% to restore to full size)

EMBROIDERY

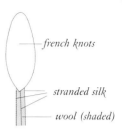

french knots

stranded silk

wool (shaded)

figure 1

Tree Using one strand of light green wool, couch the trunk of the tree. Using two strands of light green Silk for the foundation thread and one strand for the couching, couch in between wool couching. Using one strand of dark green wool, work 1-wrap french knots to form the top of the tree (figure 1).

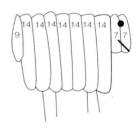

figure 2

Sheep Using two strands of cream wool and a size 1 straw needle, work seven 14-wrap bullion stitches. The head is two 7-wrap bullion stitches, worked side by side. The tail is one 9-wrap bullion stitch. Using two strands of black wool, work straight stitches for the legs. Using one strand of black wool, work a 1-wrap french knot for the eye and a straight stitch for the mouth (figure 2).

Hollyhocks All the hollyhocks are worked in one strand of Silk thread and a size 7 straw needle. Using dark pink Silk, work seven blanket stitch pinwheels, gradually getting smaller as you reach the top. Work one 2-wrap french knot and two 1-wrap french knots at the very top. Using one strand of gold Silk, work 1-wrap french knots in the centres. The amount will depend on the size of the pinwheel. To the left of the dark pink hollyhock, work three blanket stitch pinwheels and four half pinwheels (so it looks like the light pink hollyhock is under the dark pink). Using one strand of dark green Silk, work fly stitch leaves either side of the dark pink hollyhock. In light pink Silk, work eight blanket stitch pinwheels with three 1-wrap french knots at the top. Using medium pink, work clusters of 1-wrap french knots in the centres of the first seven. Using medium pink Silk, work nine blanket stitch pinwheels and two 2-wrap french knots and three 1-wrap french knots at the top. Using dark pink silk, work clusters of 1-wrap french knots in the centres. Using light green silk, work fly stitch leaves either side of the two hollyhocks.

Lavender Using one strand each of the purple cottons and one strand of green cotton threaded into a size 7 straw needle, work 1-wrap french knots underneath the sheep.

Small Daisies Using one strand of white Silk, work five petal daisies in lazy daisy stitch (see 'Shaping daisies' on page 18). Using one strand of yellow Silk, work a 1-wrap french knot in the centre. There are five with only two petals and a centre.

Large Daisies Using one strand of blue wool, work 5-petal daisies in lazy daisy stitch. Using one strand of yellow silk, work a 1-wrap french knot in the centre.

Detail: Sheepish Wheat Bag

Yellow flowers Using two strands of yellow Silk, work three satin stitches for each petal. In one strand of yellow Silk, work a lazy daisy stitch around each petal. Using two strands of light green Silk, work two straight stitches for the stems.

Grass Using one strand of light green wool, work clusters of straight stitches for the grass.

figure 1

Butterfly Using one strand of gold Silk, work a 10-wrap bullion stitch for the body, and two pistil stitches for the antennae (figure 1). About 2 mm away from the body, work the first pair of wings. Using one strand of dark pink Silk and a size 9 straw needle, work one 14-wrap bullion loop stitch and one 10-wrap bullion loop stitch. Couch the wings down (figure 2). Using two strands of dark purple, work a 2-wrap french knot in the larger wing, and a 1-wrap french knot in the smaller wing. In the gap between the body and the first pair of wings, work another pair of wings in a 10-wrap and 14-wrap bullion stitch (as above). Do not couch down; the second pair of wings stand up (figure 3).

figure 2

figure 3

FINISHING

Place right sides together of the two wool pieces, then pin and tack. Remove pins and machine stitch all the way around, leaving a small opening to turn it through. Cut two pieces of dark pink braid and two pieces of light pink braid 51 cms long. Hand-stitch to the edge of bag with the ends turned under 1.5 cm, so 0.5 cm overlaps the edges. Then cut two pieces of dark pink braid and two pieces of light pink braid 23 cms long. Hand-stitch to the short ends of the bag, overlapping the longer pieces in the same way as above. Fill the bag with wheat and cloves; do not over fill. Slip-stitch the opening closed. When you want to use, microwave on high for no longer than two minutes, less if you have a very powerful microwave oven. Check the power strength of the microwave first, and **do not** overheat.

Nicholas's Dreamtime

This gorgeous framed piece creates the perfect border for a child's verse or nameplate.

- 40 cm x 45 cm blue aida fabric or heavy cotton
- Madeira Stranded embroidery cotton
  black (2400)
  white (2401)
  brown (1911)
  cream (2101)
  dark brown (2008)
  gold-brown (2104)
  tan (2012)
  orange (0114)
  grey (1802)
  red (0509)
  blue (0912)
  bright green (1204)
  yellow (0113)
  dark pink (0703)
  light pink (0607)
  purple (0904)
  grass green (1508)
- Madeira Metallic thread 9805 in
  silver (5010)
  gold (5017)
- Madeira Glamour No 8 in
  silvery white (2400)

EQUIPMENT

- Size 1 and 7 straw needles
- Doll needle

STITCHES USED

· Back stitch, bullion stitch, bullion loop stitch, chain stitch, couching, fly stitch, french knot, lazy daisy stitch, loop stitch, pistil stitch, straight stitch, satin stitch

PREPARATION

Overlock the edges of fabric. Draw a rectangle 16 cm x 20 cm onto centre of the fabric. You need lots of excess fabric for stretching and mounting the work. Put markings where you will place the bullion animals and objects. It is easier to do this than trace them all on.

EMBROIDERY

The boats, cars, cats, dogs, horses, mice, bear, penguin and rabbit are all worked in six strands of cotton and a size 1 straw needle. The bees, butterflies, fish and flowers are worked in three strands of cotton and a size 7 straw needle.

Cars Work three cars across the bottom of the rectangle in red, blue and bright green. The car body is made up of three 30-wrap bullions, worked with the doll needle. Couch each one down in two places. Using the size 1 straw needle, work three 8-wrap bullion stitches for the windows and one 12-wrap bullion stitch for the roof. Using six strands of yellow cotton work a 1-wrap french knot for the headlight. The wheels are two 12-wrap bullion loops, worked in six strands of black thread. Couch each wheel down with one strand of black thread. Using four strands of silver, work a 1-wrap french knot in the centre of the tyres. Using two strands of black thread, work two straight stitches for the steering wheel, in the shape of a T.

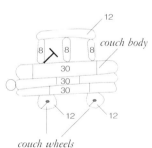

couch body

couch wheels

Boats Using red thread, work one 14-wrap bullion stitch at the base of boat, one 16-wrap bullion stitch above that and one 18-wrap bullion stitch above the last one. In blue thread, work one 20-wrap bullion stitch on top. Using red thread, work one 16-wrap bullion stitch for the mast. Using white thread, work straight stitches to shape the sails, then fill in with satin stitch. Using three strands of white, work chain stitch for the anchor. Using three strands of blue, work one 8-wrap bullion stitch and one 16-wrap bullion stitch. In one strand of blue, couch the centre of the 16-wrap bullion stitch to create the anchor shape.

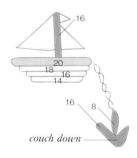

couch down

Cats The cat in the lower left corner is worked in orange and white and the cat on the right is black and white. Work from the outside of the body in. Using black or orange thread, work two 22-wrap bullion stitches and two 20-wrap bullion stitches. The tummy is worked in white thread. Work two 16-wrap bullion stitches and one 10-wrap bullion stitch. The head is two 11-wrap bullion stitches on the outside and two 7-wrap bullion stitches in the centre. The ears are two straight stitches, worked into a point, in six strands of orange or black, with one straight stitch of pink in the centre. The legs are two 8-wrap bullion stitches and the tail is one 16-wrap bullion stitch. Couch the tail into shape with one strand of the same colour thread. The front feet are lazy daisy stitches and the paws are three 1-wrap french knots. The eyes are worked in three strands of black (orange cat) or white (black cat) and are formed with two 1-wrap french knots. The nose is a 1-wrap french knot, worked in three strands of light pink. The whiskers are two straight stitches, worked in the Glamour thread.

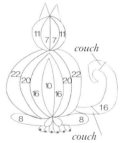

couch

couch

NICHOLAS'S DREAMTIME TEMPLATE—70%

(Enlarge to 143% to restore to full size)

KEY   Butterfly   Rosebuds

Bee   Daisies

Dogs The dog on the left is white and the dog on the right is dark brown.

The body is three 10-wrap bullion stitches. The long legs are 12-wrap bullion stitches and the short legs are 7-wrap bullion stitches. The top of the neck is one 7-wrap bullion stitch and the bottom is one 5-wrap bullion stitch. The head is two 7-wrap bullion stitches that join at the nose but are apart at the neck. Inside of this is one 5-wrap bullion stitch. The ears are also worked in six strands and are two straight stitches worked into a point (fill the centre with a small straight stitch if necessary). The eye and mouth are worked in three strands of thread, black for the white dog and light pink for the brown dog. The eye is a 1-wrap french knot and the mouth is straight stitch. The tail is one 12-wrap bullion stitch; as it is quite curved you may need to couch it down with one strand of the same colour thread. The brown dog has a 5-wrap bullion stitch tongue in three strands of light pink.

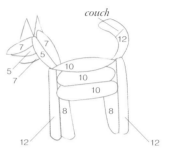

Mice There is one black mouse, one grey mouse and two white mice.

The body has two 14-wrap bullion stitches on the outside, two 12-wrap bullion stitches inside of these and one 8-wrap bullion stitch in the centre. The ears are two 12-wrap bullion loop stitches. The tail is one 20-wrap bullion stitch, that is couched down in two places with one strand of thread in the same colour to shape it. The nose is a 1-wrap french knot in six strands of light pink. The whiskers are worked in the Glamour thread and are three straight stitches.

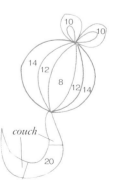

Rabbit The rabbit is worked in brown (1911) and cream. The head has two 9-wrap bullion stitches on the outside and one 7-wrap bullion stitch inside of these. The body has two 20-wrap bullion stitches on the outside, two 18-wrap bullion stitches inside of these and one 14-wrap inside of these. The tail is worked in six strands of cream. Fasten thread on the back and come through to the front, make a loop by going back through to the back and fastening off. Do not cut the thread. This leaves a 1cm loop on the front. Do this eight times, fastening each loop off. When you have finished, cut off the tops of the loops and you will have a fluffy tail.

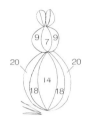

Penguins The penguins are worked in black and white. The body has two 14-wrap bullion stitches on the outside worked in black. The tummy is worked in white and has two 11-wrap bullion stitches. The head is in black and has two 9-wrap bullion stitches worked side by side. The flippers are worked in black in lazy daisy stitch. The eyes and the beak are worked in three strands of yellow. The eyes are one 1-wrap french knots and the beak is two straight stitches worked into a point.

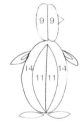

Horse The horse is worked in tan (2012) and cream. The body is worked in tan and has three 12-wrap bullion stitches. The longer back leg is one 14-wrap bullion stitch and the two shorter legs are one 7-wrap bullion stitch each. The front leg and neck are one bullion that is 22 wraps. Couch this down in one strand of tan so it bends at the knee. The neck also has a 7-wrap bullion stitch beside the long bullion. The bottom of the head has two 7-wrap bullion stitches and the top has one 5-wrap bullion stitch. The ears are two straight stitches worked into a

couch

point. The mane and tail are worked in cream. For the mane, fasten thread on the back and come up on the edge of the neck. Make a loop by taking a stitch right next to where you came up through to the back, leaving a small loop on the front, and fasten off. Go back through to the front just next to the first loop and make another loop in the same manner. Work five loops altogether for the mane. The tail is worked the same as the rabbit, except you cut loops in half. The eyelashes are two straight stitches in three strands of black. The hooves are 1-wrap french knots in six strands of black.

Fish Each fish is worked in two colours, one for the body and tail and another for the inside of the tail and eye. The body has two 9-wrap bullion stitches on the outside and one 7-wrap inside of these. When working the outside two bullions, leave a small gap at the mouth end. The tail is two lazy daisy stitches with a straight stitch worked inside of each one in a contrast colour. In the same colour work a 1-wrap french knot for the eye.

Bear The bear is worked in six strands of gold-brown and cream. In gold-brown, work two 9-wrap bullion stitches for the outer head of the bear. Inside of these work two 7-wrap bullion stitches. The ears are two 12-wrap bullion loops, couched down with a single thread. Work a one-wrap french knot in the centre of each in cream. The outside of the body is two 14-wrap bullion stitches. In cream, work two 11-wrap bullion stitches for his tummy. In gold-brown, work two 7-wrap bullion stitches for each arm. The legs are two 8-wrap bullion stitches each and the feet are one 5-wrap bullion stitch. In three strands of black, work two 1-wrap french knot eyes and one for his nose.

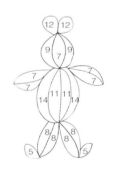

Butterflies   The butterflies are worked in three colours each: bright yellow for the body and antennae and two colours for the wings. The larger wings are two 18-wrap bullion loop stitches and the smaller wings are two 12-wrap bullion loop stitches. Couch each wing down with one strand of the same colour cotton. In another colour, work a 1-wrap french knot inside each of the smaller wings and one 5-wrap bullion stitch inside the larger wings. The body is one 11-wrap bullion stitch worked in yellow. Start the bullion at the top of the butterfly, so that when you are pulling it through you can pull it very tight, so that the tail end is thinner. Work each antennae in pistil stitch.

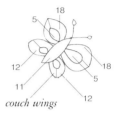

couch wings

Bees   The bees are worked in yellow, black and the Glamour thread. I thread up two needles, one in black and one in yellow. Start at the top of the bee. In yellow, work a 7-wrap bullion stitch, and just below this work another 7-wrap bullion stitch in black. Just below this work a 5-wrap bullion stitch in yellow and then one in black. Just below this work a 3-wrap bullion stitch in yellow and then one in black. In black, work two 1-wrap french knots just above the yellow 7-wrap bullion stitch for the eyes. The wings are four lazy daisy stitches worked in the Glamour thread.

Seagulls   These are worked in white and black. In white, work two 9-wrap bullion stitches that curve. In black, where the wings meet, work two tiny straight stitches for the beak.

Flowers The roses are worked in dark pink and are two 7-wrap bullion stitches. The leaves and stem are worked in dark green, using straight stitches for the stems and lazy daisy stitches for the leaves. The daisies are worked in white and purple with yellow centres. The petals are five lazy daisy stitches and the centre is a 1-wrap french knot. The stems are straight stitches and the leaves are lazy daisy stitches worked in green. The grass is worked in straight stitch in green. If you like, you can embroider your name in the corner in back stitch in gold metallic thread.

FINISHING

I had mine professionally framed.

Detail: Nicholas's Dreamtime

Playtimes, Funtimes Rug

This gorgeous blanket would also make a lovely wall hanging or playrug.

MATERIALS

- 1m x 1m cream doctor's flannel
- 4.2 m green satin blanket binding
- 4 m of 15 mm green and blue tartan ribbon
- 1 m x 1 m cotton tartan to match
- 1m x 1 m wadding
- Madeira Stranded cotton
  yellow (0113)
  black (2400)
  red (0511)
  dark blue (0913)
  light blue (0909)
  bright green (1305)
  green (1204)
  dark green (1313)
  light green (1702)
  grey (1801)
  white (2401)
  brown (1912)
  gold-brown (2204)
  cream (2101)
  tan (2012)
  pink (0605)
  flesh pink (0501)
  pale yellow (0112)
- Madeira Metallic thread 9805 in
  silver (5010)
- Madeira Rainbow Glissen Gloss in
  orange (27)
  gold (25)
- Sewing thread to match ribbon

EQUIPMENT

· Size 1 and 7 straw needles
· Doll needle
· Sewing machine

STITCHES USED

· Bullion stitch, bullion loop stitch, running bullion stitch, bullion lazy daisy stitch, couching, french knot, back stitch, stem stitch, straight stitch, satin stitch, running stitch, loop stitch, pistil stitch, chain stitch, fly stitch

PREPARATION

The template for this project is on the pull-out sheet at the back of this book. Tack the tartan ribbon onto the flannel in squares 33 cm apart, to create nine squares. Machine-stitch the ribbon in place by stitching down on either side of the ribbon. Remove tacking thread.

EMBROIDERY

Use the size 1 straw needle for embroidery in six strands, the size 7 straw needle for embroidery in three strands and the doll needle for bullion stitches longer than 20 wraps.

Boat panel In six strands of blue 0913 work three rows of backstitch for the sea. The boats are worked in six strands of thread, one yellow and green 1204, one red and yellow and one green 1204 and red. The sails are six strands of white. The base of the boat is one 14-wrap bullion stitch, and above this is one 16-wrap bullion stitch, one 18-wrap bullion stitch and one 20-wrap bullion stitch. In another colour work a 22-wrap bullion stitch on top. The mast is the same colour as the base and is one 16-wrap bullion stitch. You may need to couch the mast and boat bullions down with one strand of the same colour thread. To shape the sail, take straight stitches to form one large triangle on the left of the mast and two triangles on the right. Fill in with satin

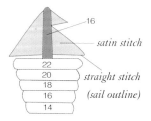

satin stitch

straight stitch
(sail outline)

stitch. The anchor chain is worked in two strands of yellow and one strand of gold and is formed by ten chain stitches. The anchor is worked in three strands of green 1204, using one 9-wrap bullion stitch and two 5-wrap bullion stitches. The seagulls are worked in three strands of white for the wings, and two strands of orange Metallic for the beak. Use two 9-wrap bullions for the wings, and two straight stitches for the beak.

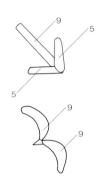

Girl Panel These are worked in six strands of thread except for the hands, bow and face, which are worked in three strands. The head is worked in flesh pink and the outside two bullion stitches have 11 wraps each. The inside two bullions have 8 wraps each. The neck is two 3-wrap bullion stitches. In pink, work three 14-wrap bullions for the jumper. Work two 12-wrap bullion stitches for each arm. The hands are in flesh and are three lazy daisy stitches. The skirt is in blue 0913 or green 1305. Work one 10-wrap bullion stitch for the waist and then one 12-wrap bullion stitch and one 14-wrap bullion stitch below the waist. The legs are worked in flesh and are one 10-wrap bullion stitch each. The shoes are worked in pink and are one 5-wrap bullion stitch each. The hair is worked in light yellow. The two outside bullions have 14 wraps each. The smaller bullions have 8 wraps each. The bow in the hair is worked in three strands of pink and is two lazy daisy stitches for the bow loops and two straight stitches for the ties. The eyes are worked in three strands of blue 0913 and are 1-wrap french knots. The mouth is three strands of pink and is a fly stitch. The grass is worked

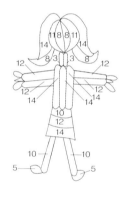

in six strands of green 1305, in straight stitches. The butterflies are worked in three strands using yellow 0113 for the bodies and pink, green 1305 and blue 0913 for the wings. The larger wings are 18-wrap bullion loop stitches and the smaller wings are 12-wrap bullion loop stitches. Couch each wing down in one strand of the same colour thread. Inside the larger wings work a 5-wrap bullion stitch and inside the smaller wings a 1-wrap french knot. The body is an 11-wrap bullion stitch and the antennae are in pistil stitch.

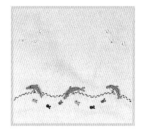

couch wings

Dolphin Panel In blue 0913, work two rows of running stitch for the sea. The dolphins are worked in six strands of white and grey. The fish are worked in three strands of yellow 0113, green 1305 and blue 0913. The seagulls are worked in three strands of white thread and two strands of orange Metallic. In grey, using a size 1 straw needle, work two 7-wrap bullion stitches for the snout. With the doll needle, work one 40-wrap bullion stitch for the top of the dolphin. Coming in at the same hole either end of the top bullion, work a 38-wrap bullion stitch. Inside of these work a 34-wrap bullion stitch. You will need to couch these into shape with one strand of thread. In white work one 20-wrap bullion stitch for the belly. The flippers are worked in grey and are lazy daisy stitches. One is on top of the body and one is worked over the top of the white bullion stitch. The tail is two lazy daisy stitches with a straight stitch worked inside each to fill in. The eye is three strands of black and is a 1-wrap french knot. The fish have two 9-wrap bullion stitches on the outside of the body and one 7-wrap inside of these. The tail

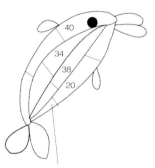

couch each bullion
as shown

is two lazy daisy stitches in the same colour. Inside each lazy daisy stitch, in a contrasting colour work one straight stitch. In the same colour work a 1-wrap french knot for the eye. The seagulls are worked the same as for the boat panel.

Koala Panel The mother koalas are worked in six strands of brown and cream. The tree is worked in six strands of green 1702. The grass is worked in straight stitch in six strands of green 1305 and the flowers are worked in 1-wrap french knots in six strands of pink. The baby koalas and bees are worked in three strands of thread. The bees are worked in yellow 0113, black, blue 0909 and gold. Work the trees first. Take three straight stitches for the trunk of the tree and couch down each stitch with one strand of thread. The branch the koalas sit on is two straight stitches couched down together. The other two branches are one straight stitch couched down. The body of the mother koala is worked first. In brown work one 36-wrap bullion stitch for the back. Coming in at the same hole either end, work one 22-wrap bullion stitch for the stomach. Inside of these work two 20-wrap bullion stitches. Couch all the bullions down with one strand of brown. For the head work two 11-wrap bullion stitches with two 8-wrap bullion stitches inside. The ears are 10-wrap bullion loops, couched down with one strand. In six strands of cream work a 1-wrap french knot inside the loop. In three strands of cream, satin-stitch over the two centre bullions. In three strands of black, work 1-wrap french knot eyes and two 3-wrap bullion stitches for the nose. The claws are two

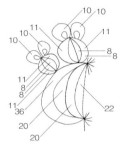

straight stitches for each claw. The head of the baby is exactly the same as the mother, except you use three strands of brown and two strands of cream and black. The bees are worked in three strands of thread. Using two size 7 straw needles, thread one with black thread and one with yellow thread. Starting at the top of the bee and in the yellow thread first, work one 7-wrap bullion stitch. Alternating the colours, work another 7-wrap bullion stitch, then two 5-wrap bullion stitches and lastly two 3-wrap bullion stitches. In black, work two 1-wrap french knot eyes on top of the yellow 7-wrap bullion stitch. In one strand of gold, work four lazy daisy stitch wings. In 3 strands of blue 0909, work running stitch for the flight path of the bee.

Bears and Balloons   The bears are worked in six strands of gold-brown and cream. The balloons are worked in six strands of yellow 0113, blue 0913, green 1305 and red. The grass is worked in six strands of green 1305. Using the size 1 straw needle, work straight stitches for the grass. In gold-brown, work two 9-wrap bullion stitches for the outer head of the bear. Inside of these work two 7-wrap bullion stitches. The ears are two 12-wrap bullion loops, couched down with a single strand. Work a 1-wrap french knot in the centre of each in cream. The outside of the body is two 14-wrap bullion stitches. In cream, work two 11-wrap bullion stitches for his tummy. In gold-brown, work two 7-wrap bullion stitches for each arm. The legs are two 8-wrap bullion stitches each and the feet are one 5-wrap bullion stitch. In three strands of black, work two 1-wrap french knot eyes and one for his nose.

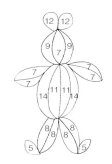

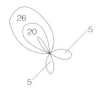

The balloons are one 26-wrap bullion loop stitch on the outside and one 20-wrap bullion loop stitch inside. Using one strand of the same colour as the balloon, couch the bullion loops at the top in the centre. The tails of the balloon are two 5-wrap bullion stitches worked in the shape of a V at the base of the balloon. The strings are in six strands of thread. Work a straight stitch across the bottom of the balloon where the tail meets the balloon. Next take a stitch from the centre of the tails to the arm of the bear. Couch this down in one strand of thread the same colour as the string.

Mice and Clock If doing this blanket again I would put the clock in the centre panel and the bears on the outside. The clock is worked in blue 0913 and green 1305. The mice are worked in grey, black and white with pink 0502 noses and silver whiskers. Trace a circle on the blanket for the clock. In six strands of green and a size 1 straw needle, work running bullion stitch around the circle. In six strands of blue, work running bullion stitch just above the green. The long hand is worked in green and is a 40-wrap bullion stitch, couched down with one strand of green, with two 5-wrap bullion stitches at the top. The short hand is one 25-wrap bullion stitch, with two 5-wrap bullion stitches at the top. The numbers are worked in six strands of blue. The one is one 3-wrap, one 9-wrap and one 5-wrap bullion stitch. The two is 14 wraps, couched down at the top, plus one 6-wrap bullion stitch. The three is two 10-wrap bullion stitches, couched down in the centre of each curve. The four is two 6-wrap bullion stitches in the shape of an L, with one 4-wrap bullion stitch over the

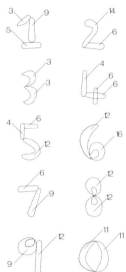

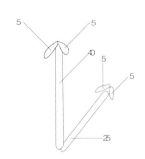

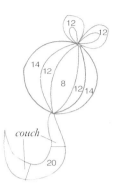

bottom bullion. The five is one 6-wrap bullion stitch at the top, one 4-wrap at the side and one 12-wrap bullion stitch at the bottom that is couched in the centre. The six is one 12-wrap bullion stitch at the side with a 16-wrap bullion loop stitch couched down in two places. The seven is one 6-wrap bullion stitch at the top and one 9-wrap bullion stitch pointing down. The eight is two 12-wrap bullion loop stitches, couched down in the centres. The nine is one 9-wrap bullion stitch and one 12-wrap bullion loop stitch, couched down in the centre. The zero is two 11-wrap bullion stitches, couched down in the centres of the curve.

The body of the mouse is worked first. The outside two bullion stitches are 14 wraps each. Inside of these are two 12-wrap bullion stitches and inside of these is one 8-wrap bullion stitch. The ears are two 12-wrap bullion loop stitches, couched down with one strand of the same colour. The tail is one 20-wrap bullion stitch, couched down in two places to get the curve. The nose is worked in six strands of pink, in the centre of the ears and is a 1-wrap french knot. The whiskers are one strand of silver and are three straight stitches.

Horse panel The horses are worked in six strands of tan and cream. For the butterflies, refer to the instructions on page 69, and to the diagram (lower right).

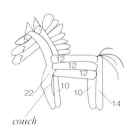

In six strands of green 1305, stem stitch the hill. The flowers are six strands of pink 0605 and are 1-wrap french knots with green straight stitch stems. The body of the horse is worked first in tan and is three 12-wrap bullion stitches. The long back leg is one 14-wrap bullion stitch. The short legs are 10-wraps each. The front leg and neck are one

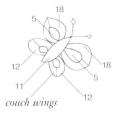

bullion of 22 wraps. Couch down at the knee to bend. The other side of the neck is one 7-wrap bullion stitch. The upper head is one 5-wrap bullion stitch and the nose is two 7-wrap bullions. The ears are two straight stitches worked into points. In cream, work a loop stitch mane and tail. Cut loops in half for the tail. The eyelashes are two straight stitches in three strands of black. The hooves are worked in six strands of black and are 1-wrap french knots.

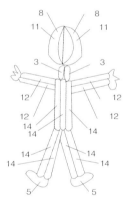

Boys and Sunflowers The boys are worked in six strands of black and red except for the hands and hair, which use three. The sunflowers are worked in three strands of yellow 0113, with two strands of Metallic orange centres and two strands of dark green 1313 for the stems and leaves. The grass is six strands of green 1305, in straight stitch. The head is worked in black, the two outside bullion stitches are 11-wraps each with two 8-wrap bullion stitches inside. The neck is two 3-wrap bullion stitches in black. The jumper is three 14-wrap bullion stitches; the centre one is black and the outside two are red. The arms are two 12-wrap bullion stitches, one red and one black. The legs are two 14-wrap bullion stitches and the feet are 5-wrap bullion stitches in black. The hands are in three strands of black and are three lazy daisy stitches. The hair is also in three strands. One boy has a row of 2-wrap french knots. The centre boy has pistil stitch hair and the third boy has two rows of 1-wrap french knots for his hair. The sunflower petals are twelve lazy daisy bullion stitches. Work four to start in the shape of a cross, then place two more stitches between each one (figure 1). The centres are filled with 1-wrap french knots in orange. The stems are stem stitch with lazy daisy leaves.

Cars and Bees Panel   The cars are worked in six strands of thread in blue 0913, green 1204, red, black, yellow 0113 and four strands of silver. The road is worked in six strands of grey and is two rows of backstitch. The bees are worked the same as in the koala panel on page 71. Stitch the road first. Using the doll needle work three 30-wrap bullion stitches for the base of the car. Couch each bullion down in two places. Using the size 1 straw needle with the black thread, work two 12-wrap bullion loops for the wheels and couch them down in the centre with one strand of black. In silver work a 1-wrap french knot for the hubcap in the centre of the wheel. The headlight is worked in yellow and is a 1-wrap french knot at the front of the top bullion stitch. The sides of the car are three 8-wrap bullion stitches and the roof is one 12-wrap bullion stitch. The steering wheel is worked in two strands of black thread and is two straight stitches in a sideways T shape.

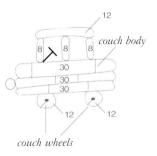

couch body

couch wheels

FINISHING

Tack wadding to blanket, then tack tartan lining to the wadding and flannel, so that the right sides are facing out. Starting in the centre of the koala panel, pin the blanket binding to the edges of the blanket, so that one side covers the front and one the back (the pins should only be about 5 cm apart). To get around the corners, fold the ribbon in on a 45-degree angle. When you get back to where you started, turn the ribbon under about 2 cm, overlapping the start of the ribbon. Carefully tack the blanket binding and then remove pins. Using a wide zig-zag stitch on your machine, sew the ribbon to the blanket. Remove the tacking thread. Another option is to hand quilt in between the tartan ribbon. I tried machine quilting and found it too thick.

Bonnie Baby Bibs

*These gorgeous baby bibs make the perfect practical gift for a new baby.
Once you have mastered these two designs, make up your own using other
embroidery patterns and motifs from this book.*

MATERIALS

for dolphin bib

- 1 blue towelling bib
- Madeira Silk thread
  white (2401)
  red (0511)
  blue (1007)
  grey (1802)
  green (1204)
  black (2400)
- medium weight interfacing

for little boy bib

- 1 cream towelling bib
- Madeira Silk thread
  black (2400)
  white (2401)
  red (0511)
- medium weight interfacing

EQUIPMENT

- Size 7 straw needle

STITCHES USED

for dolphin bib

- Bullion stitch, straight stitch, satin stitch, couching, french knot, lazy daisy stitch, backstitch, chain stitch

for little boy bib

- Bullion stitch, pistil stitch, french knot, straight stitch, lazy daisy stitch

PREPARATION

Tack interfacing to the back of the bib, where you will embroider.

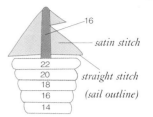

satin stitch

straight stitch
(sail outline)

EMBROIDERY

for little boy bib The boys are worked in two strands of black and red, except for the eyes and mouth which are worked in one strand. Follow the instructions on page 74, except work all the hair in pistil stitch.

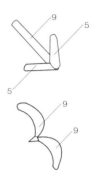

for dolphin bib In two strands of blue, work a row of backstitch for the sea. The boats are worked in four strands of thread, blue and red. The sails are four strands of white. The base of the boat is one 14-wrap bullion stitch, then one 16-wrap bullion stitch, then one 18-wrap bullion stitch, all in red. Above these is one 20-wrap bullion stitch in blue, then one 22-wrap bullion stitch in red. The mast is in blue and is one 16-wrap bullion stitch. To shape the sail, use straight stitches to form a large triangle on the left of the mast, and two triangles on the right. Fill in with satin stitch. The anchor chain is worked in one strand of green in chain stitch. The seagulls are worked in two strands of white thread and one strand of black for the beak. The wings are two 9-wrap bullion stitches and the beak is two small straight stitches. The anchor is worked in two strands of green, using one 9-wrap bullion stitch and two 5-wrap bullion stitches. The dolphins are worked in two strands of grey and white, with one strand of black for the eye. In grey, work two 7-wrap bullion stitches for the snout. Work one 40-wrap bullion stitch for the top of the dolphin. Coming in at the same hole either end of the

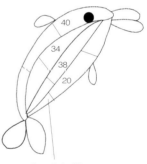

*couch each bullion
as shown*

40-wrap bullion, work a 38-wrap bullion stitch. Inside of these work one 34-wrap bullion stitch. Couch into place with one strand of grey. In white, work one 20-wrap bullion for the belly. In grey, work two lazy daisy stitches for the tail with a straight stitch inside to fill in. Work one lazy daisy stitch on top of the dolphin, and one at the bottom over the top of the white bullion. The eye is a 1-wrap french knot.

FINISHING

Cut away excess interfacing from the back of each bib.

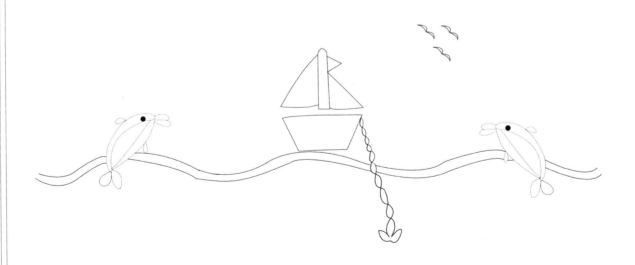

DOLPHIN BIB TEMPLATE —90%

(Enlarge to 111% to restore to full size)

Stitch Glossary

Starting and Finishing

You can use knots to start and finish. However, remember that unless it is a huge knot it will probably end up on the front of your work. I suggest starting the same way as you would finish, with two little back stitches on the back of your work (see below). Split the first stitch with the second to secure.

Back Stitch

Back Stitch is used for outlines, and appears as a continuous line. It is also used for starting and finishing.

Bring the needle up at A. Take the needle into the fabric at B and re-emerge at C (in front of A). Pull through to complete the first stitch. The distance between A and B and A and C should be the same (figure 1). Take the needle back to A, in the same hole, and come out at D, so you are always taking one stitch back and one stitch forward (figure 2). To end off, take the needle through the hole at the end of the last stitch .

Blanket Stitch

This stitch was traditionally used to finish the edges of blankets. It can be worked in a line, circle or even heart (see Pinwheel Blanket Stitch below).

Bring the needle up at A. Take the needle into the fabric at B and re-emerge at C with the thread under the needle. Pull through to complete first stitch (figure 3). Take the needle in at D and out at E, keeping the spaces between the stitches even and the vertical stitches straight (figure 4) and continue to work the row (figure 5). To end off, take the needle to the back just over the last loop. To come up again, bring the needle up to where the thread was before you finished.

Pinwheel Blanket Stitch

If working in a circle (or heart-shape), draw a circle (or heart) and mark the centre. Bring the needle up at A (always start on the outside of the circle or heart). Take a stitch from the centre (B) to C (to the left or right of A), with the thread under the needle. Pull through to complete the first stitch (figure 6). Continue working from the centre to the outside edge (figure 7), turning the fabric as you go until the circle is complete. End off the same as for blanket stitch (see above).

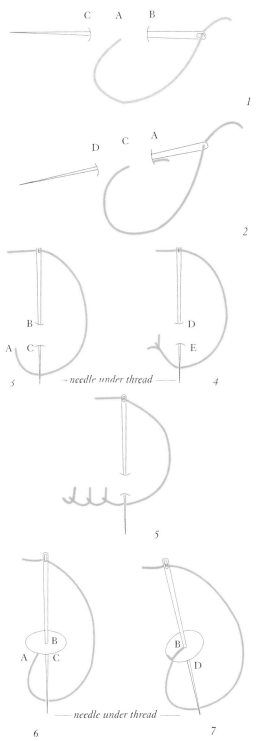

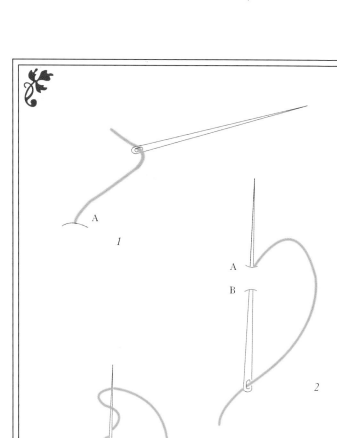

1

2

3

B

4

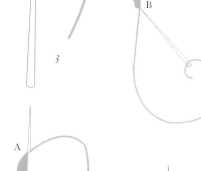

A

C

5

A

B

6

7: Bullion bud with three bullions; do outside bullions first.

Bullion Stitch

Bullion stitch is a versatile stitch which can be used on its own or in groups to form flowers, animals or people. Bring the needle up at A. This will be the start of your bullion stitch (figure 1). Take the needle in at B (the length of this stitch will be the length you want the bullion to be), and re-emerge at A, right next to the thread without splitting it (figure 2). With your left thumb over the eye of the needle and your index finger under the needle, wrap the thread clockwise around the needle (figure 3). If you want a straight bullion, the wraps on the needle should be the same length as the stitch you have taken. If you want a curved bullion the wraps on the needle should be longer than the stitch taken. The longer the wraps on the needle are in comparison to the stitch taken, the more the bullion will curve. Place your left thumb over the wraps, so you are holding onto the wraps with your index finger and thumb. Holding firmly, pull the needle away from you and through the wraps. Keeping hold of the wraps, pull all the way through and then pull back towards you. If the wraps are not even, pull the thread while rolling the wraps clockwise. To end off, take the needle to the back at B, to anchor (figure 4). If you have trouble pulling the needle though the wraps, roll the wraps anti-clockwise on the needle. This will loosen the wraps and enable you to pull through. Once you have pulled the needle through, roll the wraps clockwise until they are firm again.

Bullion Bud

Work the first bullion stitch as above. Bring the needle up at A, in the same hole at the top of the first bullion stitch without splitting thread. Take a stitch in at C, in the same hole at the bottom of the first bullion stitch (figure 5). Work the same number of wraps as before.

End off by taking the needle to the back of your work. If you want to put a bullion in the centre of the bud, work the outside bullions first with extra wraps so they sit curved on the fabric, leaving a space in the centre. Come up inside the bullions (A) as close to the end as you can, and take a stitch from the other end (B) inside the bullions (figure 6). The centre bullion will have two less wraps than the first two. If you are putting two bullions inside, they will have three less wraps each.

Large Bullion Rose

Always use the darkest colour for the centre and shade out to your lighter colours as you go.

Start in the centre, work your first three bullions in dark thread as for the bullion bud. Give the first two bullions seven wraps each and the centre five wraps. Thread with medium colour. Bring the needle out at A (in the centre of the first three and coming up just under the top bullion — figure 1). Take a stitch in at B, just below the end of the centre bullions, and go back to A (figure 2). This bullion will have nine wraps (two more than the outside centre bullions). End off at B and come up half-way above the bullion you have just made (C — figure 3) Take a stitch from D (half the size of the bullion from the end of the last bullion) and go back to the thread C (figure 4). This bullion will have eleven wraps. End off and come up half-way above the bullion you have just made. Working clock-wise, continue working around in the same way, in-creasing the wraps by two until you get back to where you started and up to fifteen wraps. Work one more bullion with fifteen wraps in the medium colour. Thread up with the lightest colour. Come up half-way above the last medium colour bullion worked. Work your way around the medium colour bullions, using fifteen wraps for each bullion. Always come up half-way above the bullion you have just created, taking a stitch half the size of the bullion from the end of it and always back to the thread to wrap.

Bullion Loop

This is the same as a bullion stitch except it forms a loop on top of the fabric. The numer of wraps will determine the size of the loop (the more wraps, the bigger the loop).

Bring the needle up at A. Take a stitch from B to A (figure 7). Place your index finger under the needle and wrap the thread around the needle clockwise. You can do as many wraps as you like. Hold the wraps between your index finger and thumb, then pull the needle through the wraps. Keep pulling until a loop is formed. You can end off at A if you want to have a loop with no gap, or you can end off at B to have a gap (figure 8) .

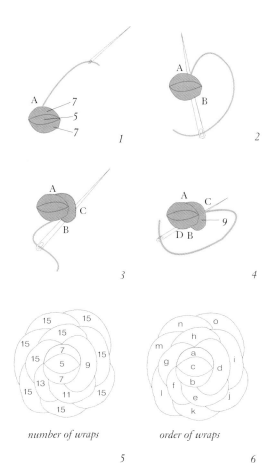

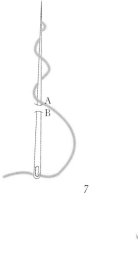

number of wraps   *order of wraps*

5   6

7

8

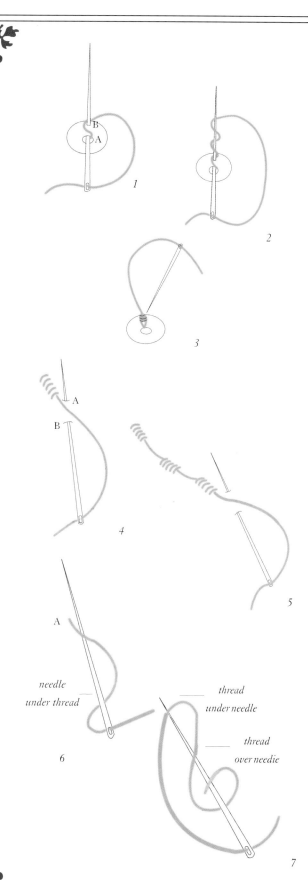

Bullion Lazy Daisy

This is a combination stitch that I use for leaves, sunflower petals and bluebells.

Bring the thread up at A. Take the needle in just to the left of A and bring it out at B (the thread is to the right of the needle). Take the thread from the right to the left, so it crosses over the needle (figure 1), and then take it under the needle and wrap it clockwise around the needle — usually two or three times (figure 2); the more wraps the longer the bullion point on the end of the lazy daisy stitch. Place your thumb over the wraps and pull the needle through the wraps away from you. End off at the end of the bullion. If you want a point at the end, take a stitch just past the end of the bullion when you end off (figure 3).

Running Bullion Stitch

This stitch looks like a continuous line of bullion stitches and is great for borders.

Bring the thread up at A. About 5 mm away, take a stitch from B back to A. Wrap the thread around the needle five times.(Of course, you can vary the length of the stitch and then the number of wraps as you wish). Pull the needle through the wraps as you would for a normal bullion stitch, but instead of taking the needle down at the end of the stitch through to the back, take a stitch back towards the end of the bullion, about 5 mm away from the end. Work another 6-wrap bullion and continue in this manner until you finish. When you run out of thread, end off as you would normally at the end of the bullion. When you come up again, come up at the same point as where you finished.

Colonial Knot

This stitch is used in candlewicking and is also known as a figure eight knot.

Bring the thread up at A. Hold the thread loosely to the left and with the needle in your right hand take the needle under the thread. With the thread in your left hand, take the thread over the needle and then under; this forms a figure eight around the needle. Take the point of the needle into the fabric just next to where you came up. Pull the wraps firmly around the needle. Keeping the thread pulled tight, pull the needle all the way through to the back.

Couching

This stitch is used to attach thread or yarn to the surface of fabric. Generally, one thread is laid on top of the fabric and another is used to 'couch' — or catch —it down.

Bring the foundation thread to the front of the fabric and lay it down in the shape you want. If it is not a straight line, you can use pins to shape it. Bring the second thread — which is usually finer — to the front, just next to the foundation thread. Take a small stitch over the foundation thread through to the back. Bring the thread up again a short distance away from the first stitch.Take a small stitch over the foundation thread. Repeat to the end,   keeping the couching stitches evenly spaced (figure 1). Re-thread the foundation thread; take it through to the back of your work and fasten off. End off the couching thread on the back of your work.

Chain Stitch

This stitch is used for outlines and filling shapes.

Bring the thread up at A. Take the stitch through the same hole to B, making sure the thread is under the needle (figure 2). Pull through until a loop is formed (figure 3). Don't pull too tightly. For the next stitch, take the needle in at the same hole as B and out to C (figure 4). The thread will always be under the needle. To end off, take the needle to the back at the end of the last loop.

Detached Chain Stitch (Lazy Daisy)

This stitch is used for leaves and flower petals.

Bring the thread up at A, and take a stitch through the same hole to B, making sure the thread is under the needle (as in figure 2). Pull through until a loop is formed; the shape of the loop will be determined by how firmly you pull. Take the needle through to the back of your work at D (figures 5 and 6).

Fly Stitch

This stitch is used for calyxes of rose buds and leaves and can be worked in a V or Y shape.

Bring the thread up at A. Take a stitch from B to C with the thread under the needle. Pull through to form a V. Take the thread to the back at D. Make this stitch as short or long as you like.This makes it a V or Y shape.

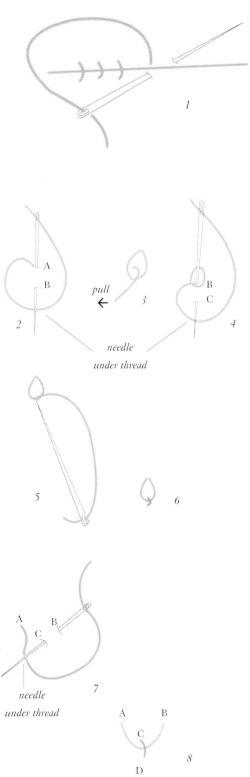

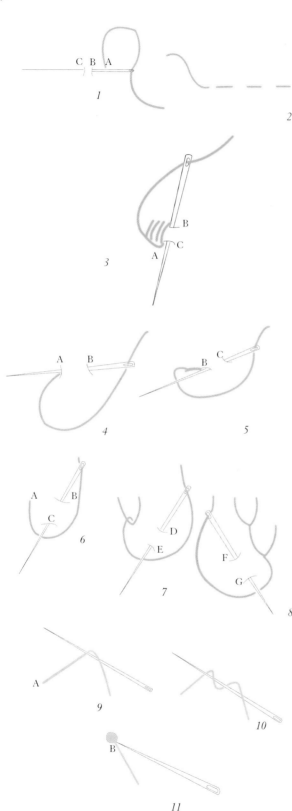

Running Stitch

This is a very easy stitch to work and is used for outlines. Mark a line on the fabric to follow. On one end of the line, bring the thread to the front at A. Take a small stitch in at B and bring out to C (figure 1). Pull through. Take another stitch in the same way, trying to keep all the stitches an even length (figure 2).

Satin Stitch

This stitch is used to fill shapes. Bring the thread out at A. Take a stitch through to the back at B. Bring the needle out again at C, as close as possible to A. Keep taking stitches that are very close to each other, so you can't see the fabric between the stitches(figure 3).

Stem Stitch

This is an outline stitch and great for stems. Bring the needle out at A. Take a stitch from B back to A, with the thread below the needle (figure 4). Keeping the thread below the needle, take a stitch from C back to B (figure 5). Keep working in this manner.

Feather Stitch

This is a delicate stitch used for foliage. It is similar to fly stitch except it is worked in a continuous line.

Bring the thread out a A. Take a stitch from B to C, with the thread below the needle (figure 6). Pull through. Holding the thread down with your thumb, take a stitch to the right from D to E, with the thread below the needle (figure 7). Pull through. Pulling the thread to the left, take a stitch from F to G, again with the thread below the needle (figure 8). Continue working this stitch from side to side (one stitch to the right, then one to the left). Finish with a stitch at the end of a loop.

Pistil Stitch

This looks like a straight stitch with a french knot on the end. It is used for flower stamens and animal antennae. Bring the thread out at A (figure 9). Holding the thread firmly in your left hand, wrap the thread around the needle twice (figure 10). Keeping a firm hold on the thread, take the needle in at B and pull through to the back.

Herringbone Stitch

This stitch is used to fill in and is the same as shadow stitch, except it is worked on the front of the fabric.

Trace the outline onto the fabric. Bring the thread up at A. With the thread above the needle, take a stitch from B back to A in the same hole (figure 1). Pull through. With the thread below the needle, take a stitch from C to A in the same hole and pull through (figure 2). With the thread above the needle, take a stitch from D to B in the same hole (figure 3). Continue to fill (figure 4), and remember to keep the thread above the needle when working a stitch on the bottom line, and below the needle when working a stitch on the top line. When working a curve, the stitches on the inside line are smaller.

French Knot

This is a raised stitch which can be used to fill shapes, and to make flowers and faces. Traditionally, it is worked with one wrap; however, you can wrap the thread more times to create a larger knot.

Bring the thread up at A (figure 5). Holding the thread firmly in one hand and the needle in the other, wrap the thread around the needle (figures 6, 7 and 8). Put the needle into the fabric just next to A, not in the same hole. Slide the wraps down the needle and pull the thread tight, so the wraps are firmly around the needle. Keeping a firm hold on the thread, pull the needle through to the back.

Loop Stitch

This is used for rabbit and horse tails, and horse manes.

Bring the thread up at A. Holding the thread down with your left thumb, fold it over your thumb to form a loop. Take a stitch to the back just in front of A, leaving a loop on top of the fabric. Fasten off on the back with one back stitch. Bring the thread up again just next to A and repeat the stitch. Fasten off each loop, making sure each time you go through to the back that you maintain the loop on top of the fabric.

For a horse mane, work in a line. For the horse's tail, work in and out in a very small circle, keeping the stitches very close together. You can cut the loops in half or leave them loopy. For the rabbit tail, work in and out in a very small circle and then cut the loops off and trim them to make a little pom pom tail.

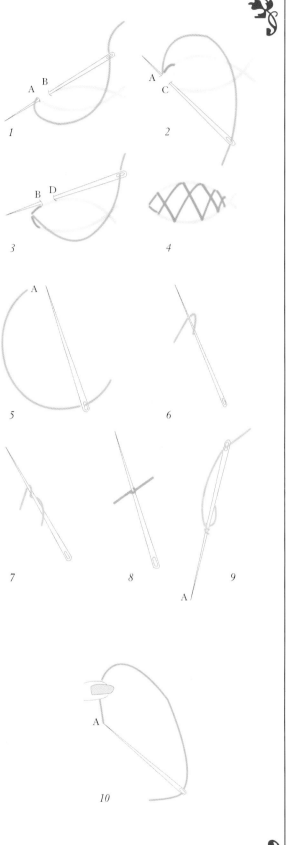

AUSSIE PUBLISHERS

AUSSIE PUBLISHERS' DISTRIBUTORS

Penguin Threads and Crafts
25 Izett Street
Prahran Vic 3181 Australia
Tel: +61-3-9529 4400
Fax: +61-3-9525 1172
Email: info@penguin-threads.com.au

Quilter's Resource Inc.
2211 North Elston Avenue
Chicago Illinois 60614 USA
Tel: +1-773-278 5695
Fax: +1-773-278 1348

Australian Folk Art Books
8 Easton Hill
Easton, nr Newbury
Berks, RG20 8ED, UK
Tel: +44-1488-608 427
Fax: +44-1488-657 757

Margaret Barrett Distributors Ltd
19 Beasley Ave
PO Box 12-034 Penrose
Auckland New Zealand
Tel: +64-9-525 6142
Fax: +64 9-525 6382

VIDEOS

Jenny Haskins
A Touch of Class — Sewing with Metallic Threads
Over the Top — Decorative Overlocking/Serging

Leisa Pownall
The A to Z of Hand Embroidery
More Embroidery Stitches and Shadow Embroidery
Animals and Flowers in Bullion Stitch
The Wonderful World of Smocking

Eileen Campbell
Machine Appliqué
Basic Free Machine Embroidery
An Introduction to Machine Quilting

Nola Fossey
Creating Wearable Art

Gabriella Verstraeten
Having Fun with Machine Embroidery
Appliqué with a Difference

Tony Barber
Tony Barber's Toy Book Video

For distribution enquiries and availability, contact:
Aussie Publishers
25-27 Izett Street
Prahran Victoria 3181 Australia
Web site: http://www.penguin-threads.com.au
Telephone +61-3-9529 4400 Facsimile +61-3-9525 1172
Email: info@penguin-threads.com.au